EXTRA DRY

WINE LIST

BOSTON
CIRACE FRANCAIS
-OR-
FRENCH
DRESSING
FOR
LADIES'AND
CHILDRENS
BOOTS & SHOES
TRUNKS, HARNESS.
B. F. Brown
BOSTON MASS.

AMERICAN CUTLERY COMPANY

FRIED
COMB
15¢

CAFÉ

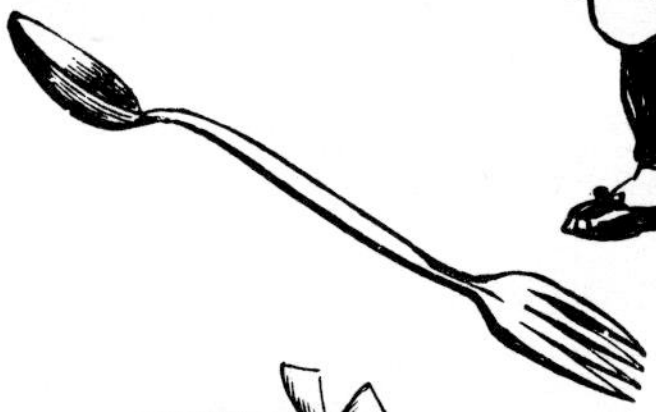

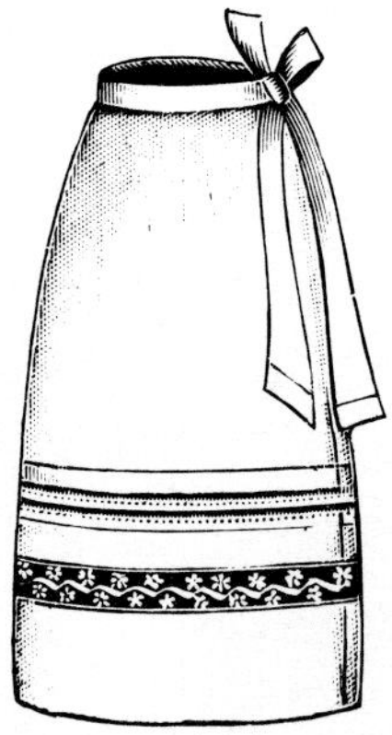

HAUT SAUTERNES
1874
BARTON & GUESTIER
BORDEAUX
FRANCE

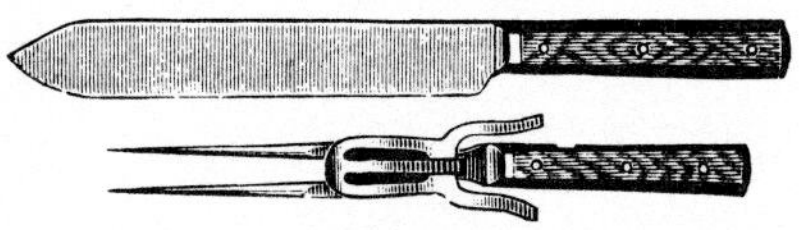

C.S.R.

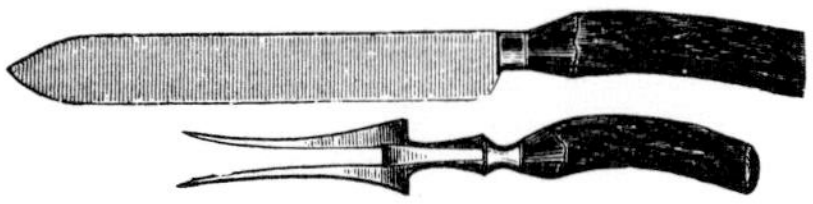

№710

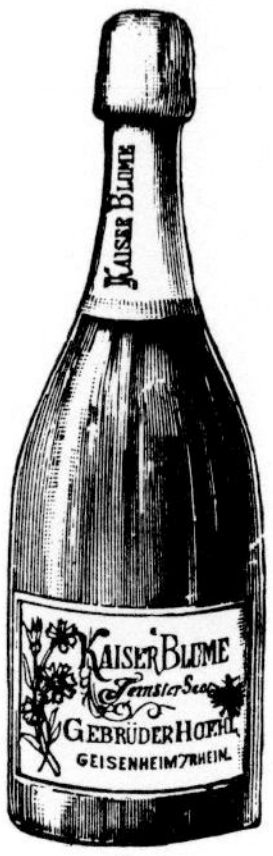
KAISER BLUME
GEBRÜDER HOEHL

RYE
COAL
YARDS

Tip Top

AMERICA'S FINEST WHISKEY
NOVENA
VERY OLD PURE RYE
Eagle Liqueur Distilleries

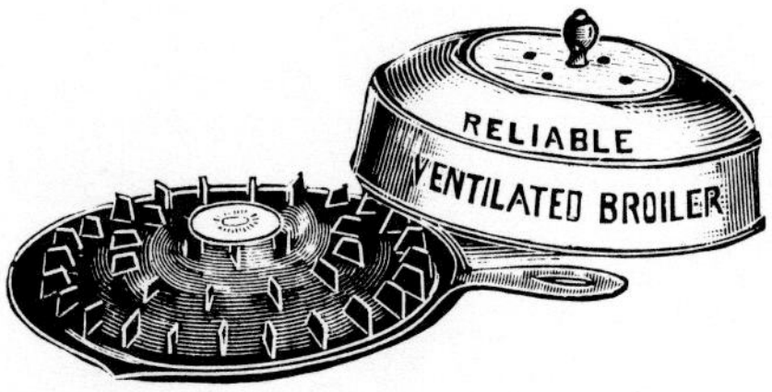
RELIABLE
VENTILATED BROILER

Rheinweine

BEURRE

Wine List

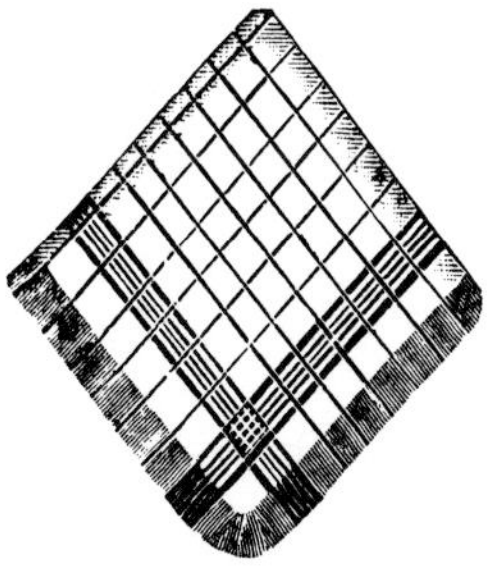

MINCE
MEAT

C.H. EVANS & SONS
INDIA PALE ALE
HUDSON, N.Y.

FREE
LUNCH
COOL
LAGER

LAGER

CHAMPAGNE
PRE MARQUE

MIXED CANDIES
FOR
SALE HERE

LE VIN

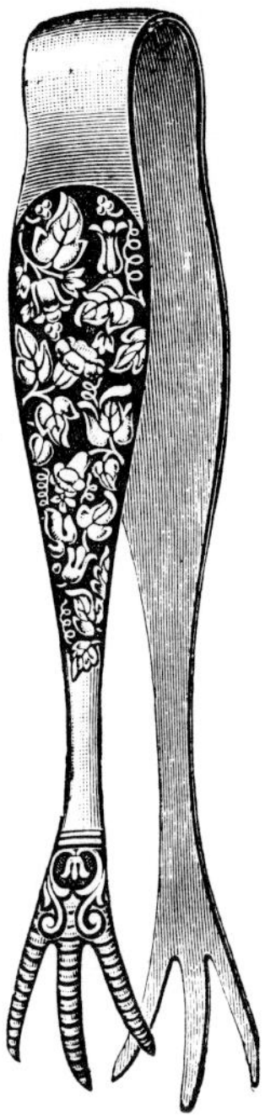

CIDRE
MOUSSEUX

GEM HONEYMOON
RYE

CARTE
du JOUR

468327
BOTTLED FALL 1912
MADE SPRING 1906
NATURAL STRAIGHT WHISKEY AGED IN WOOD
OLD
WHISKEY
BOTTLED IN BOND
OF U.S. GOVERNMENT INSPECTORS
THE SUNNY BROOK DISTILLERY CO.
JEFFERSON COUNTY, KENTUCKY, U.S.A.

SUCCOTASH

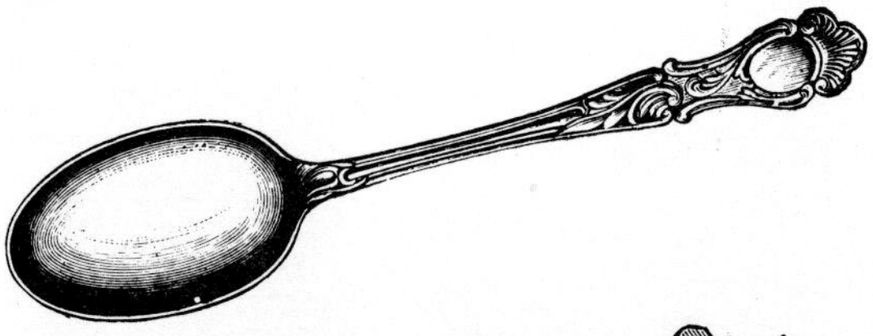

VÉLOUTÉ
AUDFROID
ESPAGNOLE
ENGALE
PERIGUEUX
BÉCHAMEL
SOUBISE
HOLLANDASE

WINE LIST.

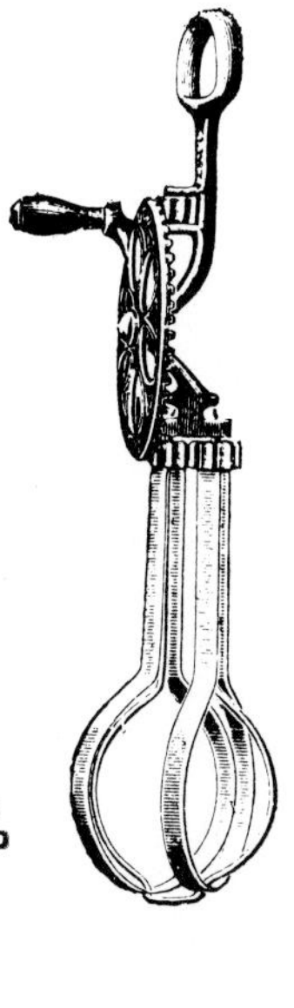

FAVORITE
BUCK-WHEAT.

Menu

GOBBLE
GOBBLE
GOBBLE
TURKEY CALL
CRANBERRY SAUCE
CELERY

PEARL WEDDING
EXTRA
SPECIAL
SELECT
RYE WHISKEY

VENTE
DE
CHARITÉ

PEARL WEDDING
EXTRA
SPECIAL
SELECT
RYE WHISKEY

PEARL WEDDING
EXTRA
SPECIAL
SELECT
RYE WHISKEY

FULL WEIGHT
ROYAL BAKING POWDER
ABSOLUTELY PURE
TRADE MARK
ROYAL
BAKING POWDER

Senf

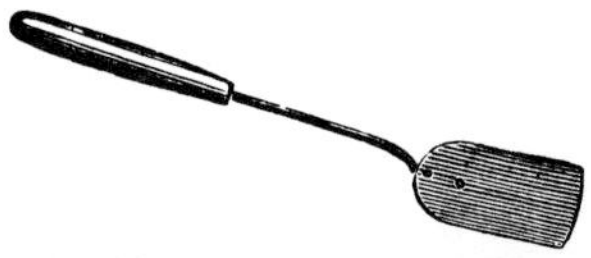

MENU

Mr PICKWICK.

WILLIAMS &
SPECIAL
RESERVE
LIQUEUR
ABERDEEN
THIS LIQUEUR WHISKY IS
YEARS OLD.

Carte du Jour

MINNESOTA
FANCY PATENT
BEST
XXXX

FULL WEIGHT PURE
DR PRICE'S
CREAM
BAKING
POWDER

FAVORITE
OLIVES

MENU

Call that 'e sole?

TEA

PONTET CANET
1887
BARTON & GUESTIER
BORDEAUX
FRANCE

HOME MADE
PIES
A SPECIALTY

BURTON
ALES

WILLIAMS & SO
SPECIAL
RESERVE
LIQUEUR
ABERDEEN

MUSTARD

MENU

Menu

Favorite Mill

C.S.R.

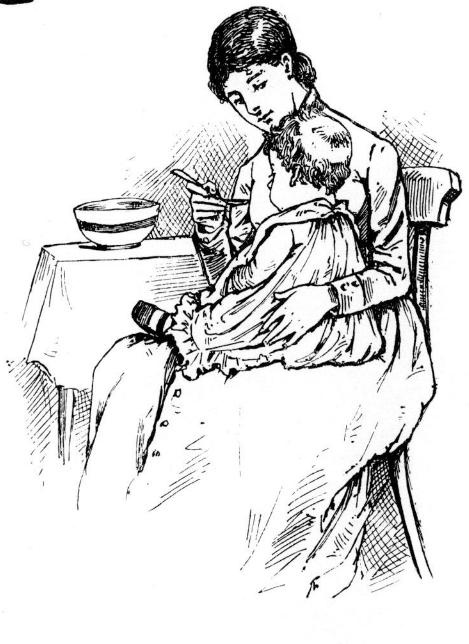

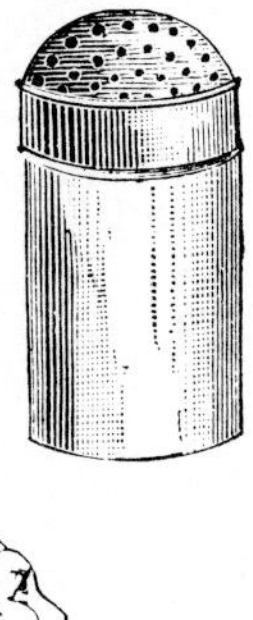

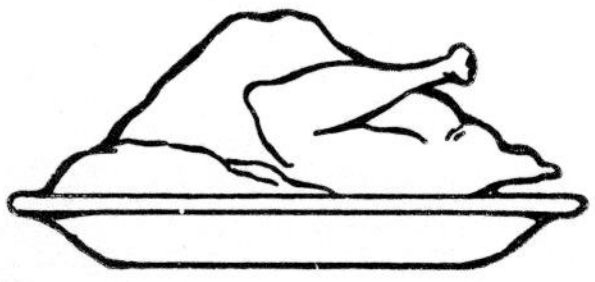

STANDARD
BRAND
TABLE SALT

PURE
VERMONT
Maple Syrup

CLAM CHOWDER - 20 cts
LOBSTER SALAD 25 cts
ICE CREAM 15 cts
TURTLE SOUP 20 cts
STRAWBERRY SHORT' CAKE 70 cts
H.P. Wolcott

PURE
GROUND
PEPPER

COLMAN'S
MUSTARD

FAVORITE
SUCCOTASH

MENU

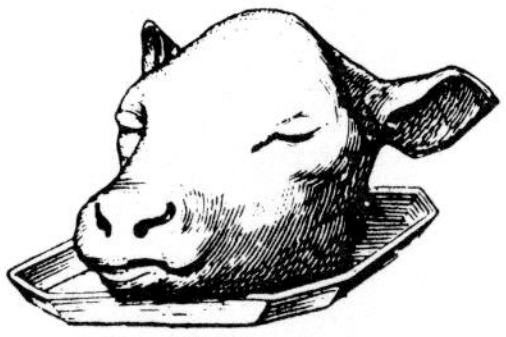

Menu

FANCY
CREAMERY BUTTER

"Their various cares in one great point combine
Menu
The business of their lives that is — to dine"
Young —

GUINNESS

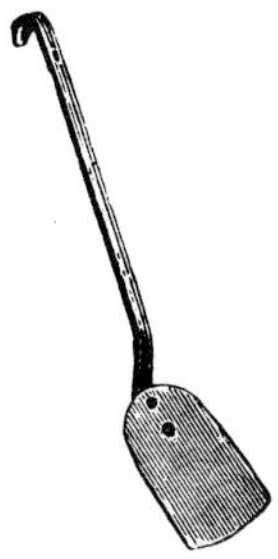

FINEST
QUALITY
CARVERS.

THE
BEER
THAT MADE MILWAUKEE FAMOUS

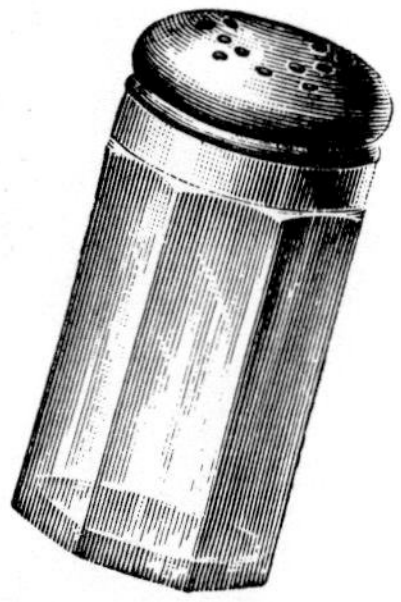

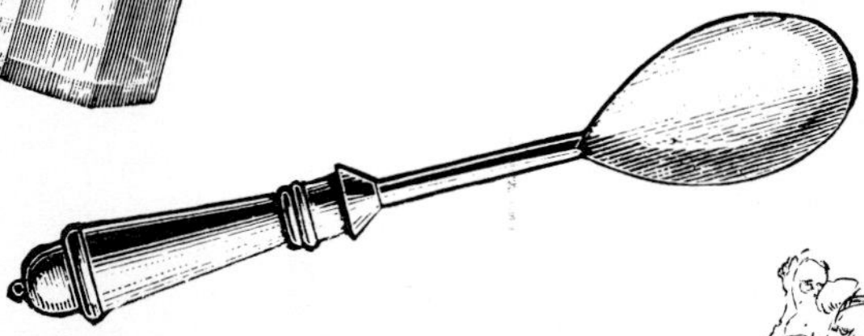

LE CAFÉ

FAVORITE
BREAKFAST FOOD

LIMONADE GAZEUSE

TEA

MENU

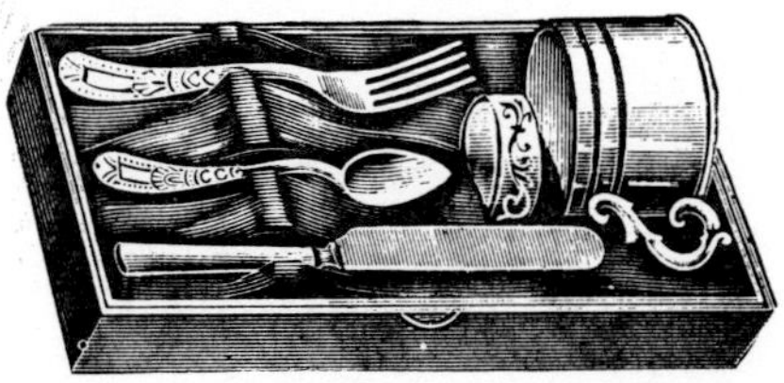

CORNED BEEF

SALAD

LA
SOUPE

MENU